The Book of Jonah

Illustrated
for children by

Niko Chocheli

ST VLADIMIR'S SEMINARY PRESS
2000

The Book of Jonah

Copyright © 2000 by
St. Vladimir's Seminary Press
575 Scarsdale Rd., Crestwood, NY 10707
1-800-204-2665

ISBN 0-88141-207-4

Scripture excerpts are taken from the New
Oxford Annotated Bible, Revised Standard
Version, copyright © 1973

The publication of this book was
made possible in part due to the generosity of
Mr. & Mrs. Mark Hudoff.

Niko Chocheli was born in Tbilisi, Republic of Georgia. He started
to draw at the age of four. Mr. Chocheli graduated with honors
from both Tbilisi Nikoladze Art College and Tbilisi State Academy
of Fine Arts. His work is reminiscent of the style of the old masters,
which he has studied for over sixteen years, and his concentration
is in Orthodox iconography. Mr. Chocheli has received many
awards for his artistic achievements throughout Europe. His work
has been exhibited in both Europe and the United States and in
many private collections. Awarded permanent residency status by
the U.S. government as "Alien of Extraordinary Abilities," Mr.
Chocheli is a associate professor of art at LaSalle University,
Philadelphia, and is a member of the Orthodox Church.

Originally published by La Salle University Museum of Fine Arts.

Cover design: Amber Houx

PRINTED IN HONG KONG

The Book of Jonah

"Then some of the scribes and pharisees said to Jesus, 'Teacher, we wish to see a sign from you.' But Jesus answered them, 'An evil and adulterous generation seeks for a sign, but no sign shall be given to it except the sign of the prophet Jonah. For as Jonah was three days and three nights in the belly of the whale, so will the Son of Man be three days and three nights in the belly of the whale, so will the Son of Man be three days and three nights in the heart of the earth. The people of Nineveh will arise at the Judgement with this generation and condemn it; for they repented at the preaching of Jonah, and behold, something greater than Jonah is here.'"
(Matthew 12:38-42; also see Luke 11:29-32)

The Gospel of Christ, with its message of mercy to all who repent for the forgiveness of their sins through the Lord's death and resurrection, is incomparably greater than the story of Jonah. Yet this prophetic tale, so charming and disarming in its simplicty and power, remains forever—by Christ's own testimony—among the unique signs of God's saving work in His beloved Son Jesus.

The prophecy of Jonah need no special commentary. Explanations of its multiple meaning often tend to ruin it. The inspired parable needs only to be read with our children, who adore it as it is. Its prophetic proclamation and messianic message will, by God's grace, reveal itself to our souls.

SVS Press is pleased to provide this illustrated version of the prophecy of Jonah especially for children. May it serve one more time, and over and again, to open our minds and hearts to the Gospel of Christ which it is inspired to prefigure and signify.

Fr. Thomas Hopko
Dean, St Vladimir's Orthodox Seminary

THE BOOK OF JONAH

Now the word of the Lord came to Jonah the son of Amittai, saying, "Arise, go to Nineveh, that great city, and cry against it; for their wickedness has come up before me." But Jonah rose to flee to Tarshish from the presence of the Lord. He went down to Joppa and found a ship going to Tarshish; so he paid the fare, and went on board, to go with them to Tarshish, away from the presence of the Lord.

But the Lord hurled a great wind upon the sea, and there was a mighty tempest on the sea, so that the ship threatened to break up. Then the mariners were afraid, and each cried to his god; and they threw the wares that were in the ship into the sea, to lighten it for them. But Jonah had gone down into the inner part of the ship and had lain down, and was fast asleep. So the captain came and said to him, "What do you mean, you sleeper? Arise, call upon your god! Perhaps the god will give a thought to us, that we do not perish."

And they said to one another, "Come, let us cast lots, that we may know on whose account this evil has come upon us." So they cast lots, and the lot fell upon Jonah. Then they said to him, "Tell us, on whose account this evil has come upon us? What is your occupation? And whence do you come? What is your country? And of what people are you?" And he said to them, "I am a Hebrew; and I fear the Lord, the God of heaven, who made the sea and the dry land." Then the men were exceedingly afraid, and said to him, "What is this that you have done!" For the men knew that he was fleeing from the presence of the Lord, because he had told them.

Then they said to him, "What shall we do to you, that the sea may quiet down for us?" For the sea grew more and more tempestuous. He said to them, "Take me up and throw me into the sea; then the sea will quiet down for you; for I know it is because of me that this great tempest has come upon you." Nevertheless the men rowed hard to bring the ship back to land, but they could not, for the sea grew more and more tempestuous against them. Therefore they cried to the Lord, "We beseech thee, O Lord, let us not perish for this man's life, and lay not on us innocent blood; for thou, O Lord, hast done as it pleased thee." So they took up Jonah and threw him into the sea; and the sea ceased from its raging. Then the men feared the Lord exceedingly, and they offered a sacrifice to the Lord and made vows.

And the Lord appointed a great fish to swallow up Jonah; and Jonah was in the belly of the fish three days and three nights.

Then Jonah prayed to the Lord his God from the belly of the fish, saying,

"I called to the Lord, out of my distress,
    and he answered me;
out of the belly of Sheol I cried,
    and thou didst hear my voice.
For thou didst cast me into the deep,
    into the heart of the seas,
    and the flood was round about me;
    all thy waves and thy billows passed over me.
Then I said, 'I am cast out from thy presence;
how shall I again look to thy holy temple?'
The waters closed in over me,
    the deep was round about me;
weeds were wrapped around my head
    at the roots of the mountains.
I went down to the land
    whose bars closed upon me for ever;
yet thou didst bring my life up from the Pit,
    O Lord my God.
When my soul fainted within me,
    I remembered the Lord;
and my prayer came to thee, into thy holy temple.
Those who pay regard to vain idols
    forsake their true loyalty.
But I with the voice of thanksgiving
    will sacrifice to thee;
what I have vowed I will pay.
    Deliverance belongs to the Lord!"

And the Lord spoke to the fish, and it vomited out Jonah upon the dry land.

Then the word of the Lord came to Jonah the second time, saying, "Arise, go to Nineveh, that great city, and proclaim to it the message that I tell you." So Jonah arose and went to Nineveh, according to the word of the Lord. Now Nineveh was an exceedingly great city, three days' journey in breadth. Jonah began to go into the city, going a day's journey. And he cried, "Yet forty days, and Nineveh shall be overthrown!" And the people of Nineveh believed God; they proclaimed a fast, and put on sackcloth, from the greatest of them to the least of them.

Then tidings reached the king of Nineveh, and he arose from his throne, removed his robe, and covered himself with sackcloth, and sat in ashes. And he made proclamation and published through Nineveh, "By the decree of the king and his nobles: Let neither man nor beast, herd nor flock, taste anything; let them not feed, or drink water, but let man and beast be covered with sackcloth, and let them cry mightily to God; yea, let every one turn from his evil way and from the violence which is in his hands. Who knows, God may yet repent and turn from his fierce anger, so that we perish not?"

When God saw what they did, how they turned from their evil way, God repented of the evil which he had said he would do to them; and he did not do it.

But it displeased Jonah exceedingly, and he was angry. And he prayed to the Lord and said, "I pray thee, Lord, is not this what I said when I was yet in my country? That is why I made haste to flee to Tarshish; for I knew that thou art a gracious God and merciful, slow to anger, and abounding in steadfast love, and repentest of evil. Therefore now, O Lord, take my life from me, I beseech thee, for it is better for me to die than to live." And the Lord said, "Do you do well to be angry?" Then Jonah went out of the city and sat to the east of the city, and made a booth for himself there. He sat under it in the shade, till he should see what would become of the city.

And the Lord God appointed a plant, and made it come up over Jonah, that it might be a shade over his head, to save him from his discomfort. So Jonah was exceedingly glad because of the plant. But when the dawn came up the next day, God appointed a worm which attacked the plant, so that it withered. When the sun rose, God appointed a sultry east wind, and the sun beat upon the head of Jonah so that he was faint; and he asked that he might die, and said, "It is better for me to die than to live." But God said to Jonah, "Do you do well to be angry for the plant?" And he said, "I do well to be angry, angry enough to die." And the Lord said, "You pity the plant, for which you did not labor, nor did you make it grow, which came into being in a night, and perished in a night. And should I not pity Nineveh, that great city, in which there are more than a hundred and twenty thousand persons who do not know their right hand from their left, and also much cattle?"

Now the word of the LORD came to Jonah the son of Amittai,
saying, "Arise, go to Nineveh, that great city, and cry against it;
for their wickedness has come up before me."
But Jonah rose to flee to Tarshish from the presence of the LORD.
He went down to Joppa and found a ship going to Tarshish;
so he paid the fare, and went on board, to go with them to Tarshish,
away from the presence of the LORD.

But the LORD hurled a great wind upon the sea, and there was a
mighty tempest on the sea, so that the ship threatened to break up.
Then the mariners were afraid, and each cried to his god;
and they threw the wares that were in the ship into the sea,
to lighten it for them. But Jonah had gone down into the inner part
of the ship and had lain down, and was fast asleep.

So the captain came and said to him, "What do you mean, you sleeper? Arise, call upon your god! Perhaps the god will give a thought to us, that we do not perish."

And they said to one another, "Come, let us cast lots, that we may know on whose account this evil has come upon us." So they cast lots, and the lot fell upon Jonah. Then they said to him, "Tell us, on whose account this evil has come upon us? What is your occupation? And whence do you come? What is your country? And of what people are you?" And he said to them, "I am a Hebrew; and I fear the Lord, the God of heaven, who made the sea and the dry land." Then the men were exceedingly afraid, and said to him, "What is this that you have done!" For the men knew that he was fleeing from the presence of the LORD, because he had told them.

Then they said to him, "What shall we do to you, that the sea may quiet down for us?" For the sea grew more and more tempestuous. He said to them, "Take me up and throw me into the sea; then the sea will quiet down for you; for I know it is because of me that this great tempest has come upon you." So they took up Jonah and threw him into the sea...

And the LORD appointed a great fish to swallow up Jonah;
and Jonah was in the belly of the fish three days and three nights.

Then Jonah prayed to the Lord his God from the belly of the fish, saying,

"I called to the Lord, out of my distress,
   and he answered me;
out of the belly of Sheol I cried,
   and thou didst hear my voice.
For thou didst cast me into the deep,
   into the heart of the seas,
   and the flood was round about me;
   all thy waves and thy billows passed over me..."

"Then I said, 'I am cast out from thy presence;
how shall I again look to thy holy temple?'
The waters closed in over me,
    the deep was round about me;
weeds were wrapped around my head
    at the roots of the mountains.
I went down to the land
    whose bars closed upon me for ever;
yet thou didst bring my life up from the Pit,
    O LORD my God..."

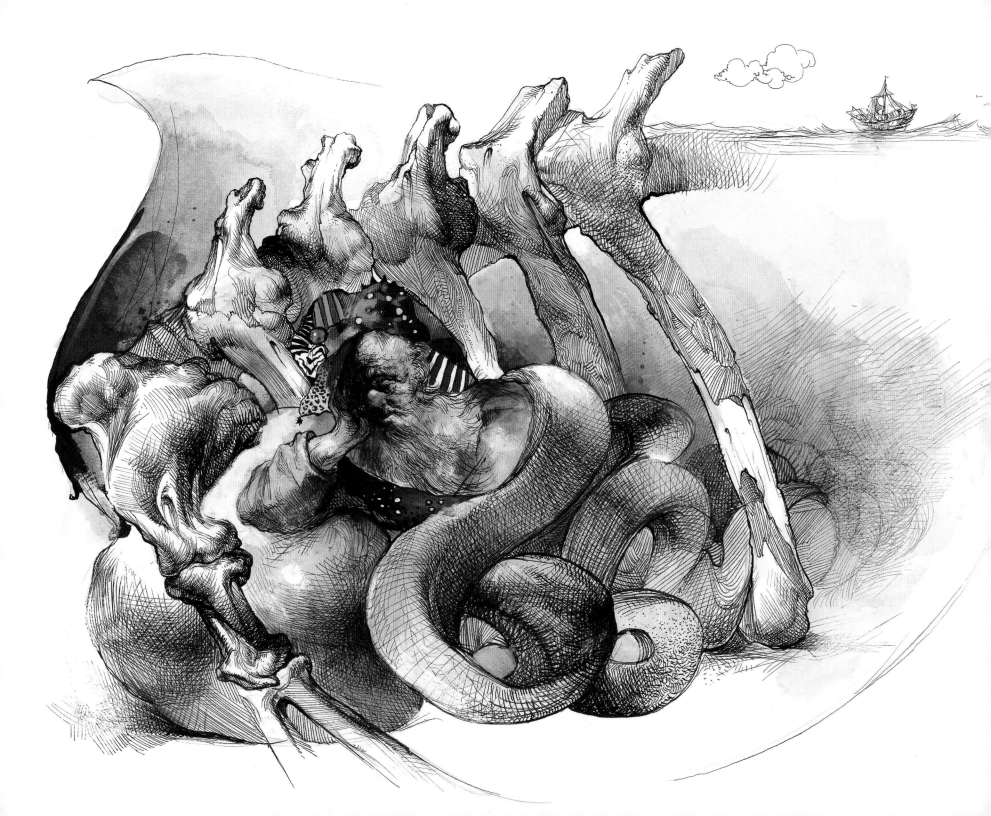

"When my soul fainted within me,
  I remembered the LORD;
and my prayer came to thee, into thy holy temple.
Those who pay regard to vain idols
  forsake their true loyalty.
But I with the voice of thanksgiving
  will sacrifice to thee;
what I have vowed I will pay.
  Deliverance belongs to the LORD!"
And the LORD spoke to the fish,
and it vomited out Jonah upon the dry land.

Then the word of the LORD came to Jonah the second time, saying, "Arise, go to Nineveh, that great city, and proclaim to it the message that I tell you." So Jonah arose and went to Nineveh, according to the word of the LORD. Now Nineveh was an exceedingly great city, three days' journey in breadth. Jonah began to go into the city, going a day's journey. And he cried, "Yet forty days, and Nineveh shall be overthrown!" And the people of Nineveh believed God; they proclaimed a fast, and put on sackcloth, from the greatest of them to the least of them.

Then tidings reached the king of Nineveh, and he arose from his throne, removed his robe, and covered himself with sackcloth, and sat in ashes.

And he made proclamation and published through Nineveh, "By the decree of the king and his nobles: Let neither man nor beast, herd nor flock, taste anything; let them not feed, or drink water, but let man and beast be covered with sackcloth, and let them cry mightily to God; yea, let every one turn from his evil way and from the violence which is in his hands. Who knows, God may yet repent and turn from his fierce anger, so that we perish not?"

When God saw what they did, how they turned from their evil way, God repented of the evil which he had said he would do to them; and he did not do it.

But it displeased Jonah exceedingly, and he was angry. And he prayed to the LORD and said, "I pray thee, LORD, is not this what I said when I was yet in my country? That is why I made haste to flee to Tarshish; for I knew that thou art a gracious God and merciful, slow to anger, and abounding in steadfast love, and repentest of evil. Therefore now, O LORD, take my life from me, I beseech thee, for it is better for me to die than to live."

And the LORD said, "Do you do well to be angry?" Then Jonah went out of the city and sat to the east of the city, and made a booth for himself there. He sat under it in the shade, till he should see what would become of the city.

And the LORD God appointed a plant, and made it come up over Jonah, that it might be a shade over his head, to save him from his discomfort. So Jonah was exceedingly glad because of the plant. But when the dawn came up the next day, God appointed a worm which attacked the plant, so that it withered.

When the sun rose, God appointed a sultry east wind, and the sun beat upon the head of Jonah so that he was faint; and he asked that he might die, and said, "It is better for me to die than to live."

But God said to Jonah, "Do you do well to be angry for the plant?"

And he said, "I do well to be angry, angry enough to die."

And the LORD said, "You pity the plant, for which you did not labor, nor did you make it grow, which came into being in a night, and perished in a night..."

"And should I not pity Nineveh, that great city, in which there are more than a hundred and twenty thousand persons who do not know their right hand from their left, and also much cattle?"

The
End